W9-CZL-895

REACHING FOR THE STARS

GARTH BROOKS
Country Music Star

Written by Rosemary Wallner

Published by Abdo & Daughters, 4940 Viking Drive Suite 622, Edina, Minnesota 55435.

Library bound edition distributed by Rockbottom Books, Pentagon Tower, P.O. Box 36036, Minneapolis, Minnesota 55435.

ISBN: 1-56239-229-8

Cover photo: Archive Photos
Inside photos: John Harrington-Black Star: 5,6,12;
            AP/World Wide Photos: 14,15,19,21,24,27,31

Edited by Julie Berg

LIBRARY OF CONGRESS CATALOGING-IN-PUBLICATION DATA
Wallner, Rosemary, 1964-
     Garth Brooks / written by Rosemary Wallner.
        p. cm. -- (Reaching for the Stars)
     Summary: Examines the life and career of the popular country musician and singer.
        ISBN 1-56239-229-8
        1. Brooks, Garth--Juvenile literature.   2. Country musicians -- United States -- Biography -- Juvenile literature.   [1. Brooks, Garth. 2. Musicians. 3. Country music.]   I. Title. II. Series.
     ML3930 . B855W3   1993
     782.42'1642'092--dc20
     [B]   93-4175
                                                                       CIP
                                                               AC MN

TABLE OF CONTENTS

A DIFFERENT KIND OF COUNTRY SINGER

From the beginning of his career, Garth Brooks wanted to be creative. He wanted to sing songs that were different. He decided to write country songs that had rock and roll beats. He decided to write slow songs that were sad, but not sappy. Fans of country music liked his ideas. In three years, Garth Brooks' fans bought 20 million copies of his records. By 1993, Brooks had sold more albums—faster—than anyone in the history of country music.

Brooks' fans love his style. They buy his albums and T-shirts. When Brooks announces a concert, fans line up to buy tickets. In Nashville, Tennessee, an arena sold all of its 10,000 tickets in 20 minutes.

Many people, including Brooks, have tried to figure out what makes him so popular. Many country singers sing as well as Brooks, so it is not just his voice that makes him a success. Brooks cares about his music and his fans. He writes songs that mean something to him and his listeners. He takes the time to meet the people who love his music. His fans say that he is pure country.

Garth Brooks' fans love his style. Garth has sold over 20 million records and his concerts sell-out in record time. Garth cares mostly about his fans.

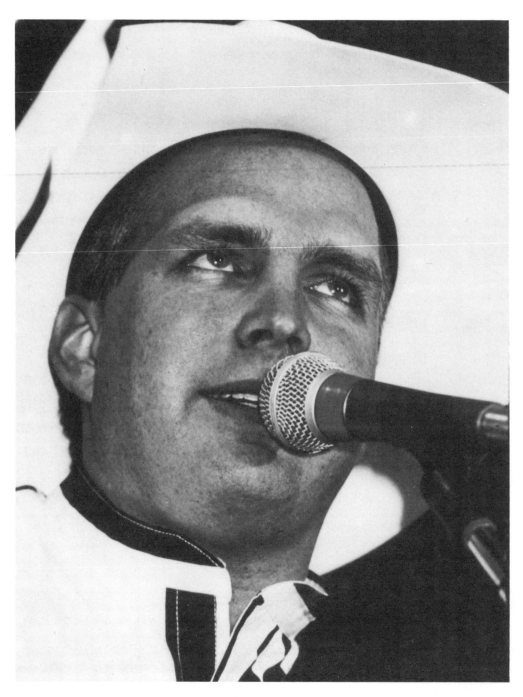

Garth's oversized, broad-brimmed hat gives him a humorous appeal.

Wearing his oversized, broad-brimmed cowboy hat, Brooks looks a little funny. But when he performs, people notice his energy and music.

Brooks pleases his country listeners, but he also has other fans. His rocking music has caught on with city slickers who love rock and roll. The popularity of his rock and roll and country style has amazed everyone. Even Brooks is surprised. In his soft Oklahoma accent he once told reporters, "Every day it is a shock."

OKLAHOMA BORN AND RAISED

Troyal Garth Brooks was born in 1962. He grew up in Yukon, Oklahoma, a small town near Oklahoma City. Brooks was the youngest of six children. His father, Raymond Brooks, was an oil company engineer. He was also an ex-marine with a short temper. But, as Brooks points out, he also had a big heart. "I learned from my father that you gotta be thankful for what you got," said Brooks. "And you gotta treat people like you want to be treated."

Brooks' mother, Colleen Carrol Brooks, had a singing career in the 1950s. She lived in Nashville and recorded albums for Capitol Records. She sang on Red Foley's "Ozark Jubilee," a popular TV show at that time. When she married Raymond, he asked her to end her career. He wanted to move to Oklahoma and raise a family. Colleen agreed.

"We kids felt that she had cut her career short because of us," said Brooks. "We wanted to carry on the tradition for her."

Brooks' large family meant that there was always someone to goof around with. "Garth was a ham as a kid," remembered his sister Betsy. "He'd do anything for the spotlight or for laughs."

Brooks has happy memories of his childhood. "Out of all the things I remember as a kid, it was the attention I remember most," he said. "I knew that someone was interested in what I was doing."

Brooks went to Yukon High School. He played sports, including football and baseball. When he was 17 years old, he learned to play the guitar. As he became interested in show business, his parents tried to talk him out of it. But from his mother he had inherited the need to perform. His music, though, would have to wait until he finished college.

COLLEGE BOUND

While Brooks was at Yukon High, he won an athletic scholarship to Oklahoma State University (OSU). He accepted the scholarship. For four years, he was a member of the track and field team. His classmates remember him as a special guy and a loyal friend. But Brooks described himself differently. "Not knowin' nothin' about a lot of stuff, that was me," he said.

At OSU, he majored in advertising and marketing. He hoped that when he graduated he could find a job writing jingles. He wanted to write the catchy tunes that people hear on radio and TV commercials. In his spare time, he played the guitar and wrote songs. In his senior year, he began to focus on performing his music.

"I stunk at everything I did," recalled Brooks. "Music was the one thing I felt proud of." His first gig was at Shotgun's Pizza Parlor in Stillwater, Oklahoma. For four nights a week he sang his songs and entertained the diners.

To help pay his bills, Brooks worked a second job as a bouncer in a nightclub. His job was to make sure the customers did not get too rowdy. One night, his boss asked him to help a young woman who had punched a hole in the bathroom wall. Brooks walked into the bathroom and met Sandy Mahl, who was also a student at OSU. Sandy had thrown a punch at another woman but had missed. Her fist had ended up in the plywood wall.

Brooks helped Sandy free her hand and told her she had to leave. As he took her outside, the two began to talk. They found that they had some things in common. Sandy and Garth began dating a short time later.

In 1985, just after he met Sandy, Brooks decided to become a singer. He thought he had enough experience singing in front of people. He was proud of the songs he had written while he was in college. He was ready to be discovered.

He packed up his guitar and his songs and headed to Nash-ville, Tennessee.

Every year, hundreds of hopeful singers head to Nashville. The city even nicknamed itself "Music City, USA" because it is a major center for recording and publishing companies. Talented singers from all over the United States travel to Nashville to record their music.

Twenty-three-year-old Brooks had two weeks of vacation. With high hopes, he traveled 600 miles east from Stillwater to Nashville. He thought that once he arrived, music executives would discover him and ask him to sign a contract. He thought it would be easy to break into the music business.

"I thought the world was waiting for me," said Brooks. "But there's nothing colder than reality." He trudged from one company to another. He introduced himself. He asked people to listen to his songs. But no one was interested. No one wanted to hear Garth Brooks' music.

Within 24 hours, he realized he wasn't ready to make it as a singer.

Years later, Brooks said that his first trip to Nashville taught him something about himself. He realized he needed more experience. He knew he had to work harder to be a singer. He knew that if he wanted to be famous, he would have to come back to Nashville someday.

"I wouldn't trade that experience for the world," Brooks said. "It was what I needed."

TO NASHVILLE—AGAIN

Brooks returned to Stillwater. Sandy cheered him up and told him that someday he would try again. With Sandy's help, Brooks kept performing with his band. He continued to write songs. He never stopped dreaming about being a singer.

In May 1986, Garth and Sandy were married. A year later, they packed up their belongings and moved to Nashville. They did not have much money, but Brooks felt that this time he was ready to become a star. On this second trip to Nashville, Brooks brought along his band, "Santa Fe". He had sung with the band while he was in college. Brooks thought that someone in Nashville might get interested in his singing and the band's playing.

Sandy worked three jobs and insisted that Brooks keep to his music. For ten months, Sandy and Garth worked together in a Nashville boot store. Whenever he had the chance, Brooks struggled to make contacts. He kept asking people to listen to his songs.

"It was fun for the first months, living with your dreams," said Brooks. "But once again reality rang the doorbell.

11

Garth Brooks has proven himself as an outstanding performer.

It just fell apart right in front of our eyes." After a few months, the members of "Santa Fe" thought it was taking too long to be discovered. They decided to leave. Even Brooks thought about quitting. He wanted to move back to Oklahoma and look for a regular job.

Sandy, however, would not let him quit. "Set a time limit of five or ten years," Sandy told Garth. "Settle down. Establish your roots. I'm not makin' this trip every year. Either we're diggin' in, or we're goin' home for good."

Brooks decided to stay and pursue a solo career. Capitol Records and every other record label rejected him, but he kept singing. Then one night he was asked to perform at a Nashville Entertainment Association show. One of the scheduled acts did not show up. Brooks was called in as a last-minute replacement.

Lynn Shults was a Capitol Nashville executive. She heard Brooks perform that night and talked to him after the show. She thought that he had talent and apologized for not listening to his tapes when he first came to Capitol. "Maybe we missed something," she told him. Shortly afterward, she asked Brooks to sign a contract with Capitol Records. Brooks was on his way to stardom.

Actor John Goodman, left, and country music sensation Garth Brooks on the set of "Saturday Night Live." The two stars hosted the March 14, 1992, edition of the show.

14

Country music singer Garth Brooks at a press conference after performing for a community project for South Central Los Angeles residents.

THE FIRST ALBUM

In April 1989, *Garth Brooks*, Brooks' first album, was ready for music stores. Capitol Records was not sure if fans would like Brooks. They only made 11,000 copies of his first album.

Brooks wrote or co-wrote about half of the songs on the album. "There's a million things you can say that need to be said," said Brooks about writing songs. "There are messages that are of common sense, of values, things people have to be reminded of."

"Much Too Young" was the first song off his album to be listed in the music industry's Top Ten list. Radio stations around the country played the tune on the air. Suddenly, Garth Brooks was the country discovery of 1989. His second single was a slow song titled "If Tomorrow Never Comes." That song hit the Top Ten in December 1989.

Brooks wrote the ballad to tell people that they should show their feelings to their loved ones. "That song means a lot to me because of friends I've lost," said Brooks. He dedicated the tune to a track coach who died in a plane crash. "Songs have to mean something to me," he added. His third single, "Not Counting You" also topped the charts.

With the success of his songs, Brooks put together a new band. He went on the road and performed wherever he could. On that first tour, he developed his stage style.

He smashed guitars and flirted with the audience. He climbed rope ladders and threw water onto his drummer. He danced back and forth around the stage, singing his heart out.

"I was losing my voice really bad because I was screaming and just kind of going nuts," said Brooks. "I stayed out all night with the guys." Brooks loved being famous. He forgot about everything else. He even became involved with another woman. Sandy found out and almost left him.

"Being true to someone carries a heavy weight on it," he admitted. "At the time I didn't think so." After his third song came out, Brooks calmed down. He was a little less rowdy. He apologized to his wife and promised to stay committed to her.

"Sandy sat me down and just said I needed to settle down—with or without her," recalled Brooks. "She wasn't going to sit around and watch me kill myself. I'm happy to be me now."

Garth Brooks kept producing hits. "Not Counting You" and "Friends in Low Places" were heard on every country radio station. "The Dance," Brooks' favorite song, was an instant hit with his fans. By September 1990, record stores had sold one million copies of *Garth Brooks*.

Each year in October, the Country Music Association (CMA) holds their awards. The CMA honors the most successful country music stars. In 1990, they gave Brooks the Music Video of the Year award for "The Dance." He was also given the Horizon Award for best new country singer. Throughout the awards ceremony, Brooks sat in the audience and held hands with Sandy. When his name was announced for the Horizon Award, he was so excited he did not let go of Sandy's hand. The two walked up on stage together. As he accepted the award he said, "I'm not much good at it, but when I don't sing, I try and be a husband. This is my wife, Sandy." The crowd cheered.

After the ceremony, reporters cornered Brooks and asked him many questions. Lights flashed as photographers took his pictures. Fans rushed up and tried to shake his hand. Brooks turned to a reporter and told him he couldn't believe that all this was happening to him. "It always seems like I'm standing outside of me," Brooks said. "Like I'm watching the whole thing go down, whatever I'm doing."

COUNTRY MUSIC'S GROWING POPULARITY

Country music is made up of songs that tell stories. Some of the stories are sad. They are about losing a loved one or leaving home. Others are happy tunes about falling in love or finding a job.

*Garth Brooks with his wife Sandy as he accepted his
awards from the Country Music Association.*

More and more people have started to listen to these country songs. Since 1980, the number of radio stations playing country music has grown. Today, more than 2,500 stations play this type of music. Garth Brooks thinks it is great that country music has become more popular. "I just think country music is finally getting what it deserves," he said. "It's the number one form of music on this planet."

No Fences, Brooks' second album, came out in August 1990. Joe Mansfield of Capitol Records made sure record stores sold the album. He paid store owners to display Brooks' posters and records. Mansfield said that many rock and roll singers pay store owners to display their records. Now that country music was becoming popular, Mansfield thought he would try the same stunt with Brooks' music.

Mansfield's idea worked. By November 1991, *No Fences* was selling 140,000 copies a month. By April 1992, it had become the best-selling country album in history.

"The Thunder Rolls" was one of the songs on this new album. It told the story of a husband who is unfaithful to his wife. The husband also abuses his wife. Brooks wanted to make a video to go along with this song. He did not want his fans to forget about this serious crime. Brooks also wanted to try acting, so he played the part of the abusive husband.

In 1991 Garth Brooks won four Country Music awards. He was also named Entertainer of the Year.

Brooks talked about the script with Sandy before he filmed the video. She was not too happy with the violent subject matter. And she did not like the fact that Brooks would be playing the bad guy. But Brooks made the video anyway.

Some people thought the finished video was too violent. The Nashville Network and Country Music Television, two cable stations, refused to air the video. They wrote letters to Brooks and complained to the newspapers about the violence. All the publicity, however, made the video—and the song—more popular.

In 1991, Brooks won four important CMA awards. He won the award for the Music Video of the Year for "The Thunder Rolls." He won Best Album for *No Fences*. He won Best Single for his song "Friends in Low Places." And he won the Entertainer of the Year Award.

When he found out he was named Entertainer of the Year, Brooks could hardly believe it. "This is cool," he said. "It's funny how a chubby kid can just be having fun and they call it entertaining."

Billboard magazine also honored Brooks. In 1991 they named him the Top Pop Album artist. As he received all these awards, Brooks never let people forget that his wife had stood beside him and helped him. "When I've been down, Sandy has given me strength," he said. "That's definitely given me what I have."

CRAZY, FUN, AND ENTERTAINING CONCERTS

Although Brooks usually writes or co-writes most of his songs, he only had time to co-write three tunes on the *No Fences* album. He was spending most of his time on the road performing for his fans.

Throughout the summer of 1990, Brooks sang with Reba McEntire. McEntire had already reached stardom as a country singer. She asked Brooks to perform as her opening act. "There are lots of artists who can sing, but who can't impart the emotion and personality that make an entertainer shine," said McEntire. "Garth pulls it off."

All that summer, Brooks worked to perfect his act. By 1991, he was ready to strike out on his own. He formed Stillwater, his own band named after the town where he went to college. He asked his sister Betsy to play the bass. He asked his brother Kelly to be his accountant. He asked his wife to travel around the country with him.

"I surround myself with people who knew me before I happened," explained Brooks. "So if I start acting differently, they'll square me in a minute."

Wild times and surprises await everyone who has a ticket to a Garth Brooks concert. For one show, Brooks might burst on stage through billows of smoke. For another, he might bounce down a stairway through multi-colored lights.

23

Brooks uses his high energy to excite his crowds. Prior to the start of Super Bowl XXVII, Brooks sang the National Anthem as actress Marlee Matlin signed.

A few times he has just walked on stage, picked up his guitar, and started singing. If the concert is sold out, the roar from the crowd can be deafening.

Throughout his concerts, Brooks uses his high energy to keep the crowd on its feet. He paces back and forth, pumping his fist in the air. As he sings, he runs from one end of the stage to another. For fun, he might climb a rope or run up and down the stage's stairs. He does anything for a response and a roar from his fans.

As people scream and yell and sing his songs, Brooks thanks the crowd. In a soft voice he says that if they don't mind, he'd like to come back next year.

Brooks prefers not to perform in large outdoor stadiums. He thinks they are too impersonal. "It's just too big," he said. "I like for people to see. I don't like to use film or the big screens because that's too much like watching television."

"Garth's intensity comes from athletics," said Mick Weber, Brooks' friend and road manager. "Once he hits the stage, it's Game Day. He's got a very competitive nature."

"The only time I know I'm really alive and doing something on God's great earth is when I'm in between those speakers and the lights are up and the music is loud," said Brooks. "I never want to get down. I never want to get off the stage."

ROPIN' THE WIND

By the fall of 1991, Brooks had two albums in the Top Ten list. *No Fences* was the number one album in the United States. When *Ropin' the Wind,* his third album, came out, it was an immediate success. By the end of September, *Ropin' the Wind* had reached the number one spot on the country and pop charts. That album was the first in country music history to climb to the top of the charts so fast. *Ropin' the Wind* began to break all of Nashville's sales records. It became the fastest-selling album in the United States.

"This has been quite a week," said Brooks after he learned that his album was number one. "I don't know if this guy deserves it."

By January 1992, *Ropin' the Wind* had already sold 3 million copies. Brooks' album was outselling all other albums. Record stores sold more Garth Brooks albums than Guns 'N' Roses and U2 albums.

When someone asked him the secret of this success, Brooks smiled shyly. He said that fans see him "as a real person, as the guy next door."

Pam Lewis, Brooks' manager, also had an answer to why this singer is so popular. "The secret to his success," she said, "is that people can relate to him. He's an Everyman. He's chubby. He's balding. Sometimes his grammar's not the best. But he's very human. I've seen him cry on stage."

*A tearful Garth Brooks is embraced by country music legend Johnny Cash,
left, as Brooks accepts his Entertainer of the Year award.*

Brooks' fans wanted to see more of their favorite performer. As a result, Brooks began appearing on television. In November 1991, he was a guest on the NBC-TV show "Empty Nest." In late 1991, he signed a contract with NBC to star in his own TV special.

Rick Ludwin, an NBC executive, loved the idea. "There is rarely a performer who explodes with the popularity that Garth Brooks has," he said at the time. "We're tremendously pleased that his first TV special will be with us."

"This Is Garth Brooks" aired on NBC on a Friday night in January 1992. Brooks sang, danced, and talked about his life and music. The show earned NBC its highest Friday night ratings in more than two years.

In March 1992, Brooks' albums were outselling even Michael Jackson's albums. "I really don't have a clue why it happened to me," said Brooks of his fame. And he kept on getting more popular. In September 1992, Brooks released *The Chase,* his fourth album. That same year he made *Beyond the Season,* his first Christmas album.

People who worked at Capitol Records could hardly believe the success of their star. Jimmy Bowen, president of Capitol's Nashville division, summed up Brooks' career so far. "Sure, Garth Brooks is great for Capitol Records," he said. "But he is also great for all of Nashville and all of country music."

Brooks ended 1992 by winning a Grammy Award for Best Male Country Vocal Performer. Again, he thanked his wife for sticking by him. "I am so thankful to God and Sandy," he said. "It turned out real well for me."

IT'S ALL WORTH IT

In April 1992, *Garth Brooks* had sold 2.5 million copies. Brooks' concerts sold out within hours. That same year, his lawyer announced that the Garth Brooks Fan Club was no longer active. The lawyer said Brooks wanted to end the fan club. The reason? Brooks could no longer meet one-on-one with each of its members.

That did not stop his fans from forming a new club called The Believers, Incorporated. This group in Tennessee publishes a magazine called *The Believer.* It is filled with information about Brooks.

Thirty-one-year-old Brooks has experienced many successes. And it has all happened in a short time. Brooks hopes he will be around awhile. "I want to be here a long time and not be a flash in the pan," he said. He also wants his fans to know that he will keep striving to be better. "Just for the record," he said, "I don't think I'm at the top."

Brooks keeps his awards and trophies out of sight. A closet in the guest room holds all these treasures.

"I've got my letters and my fans," he explained. "These are the real trophies."

When he goes on tour again, Brooks plans to stay awhile in cities where concerts have been sold out. He will bring his family and stay in one city for two, three, or four nights. He said he would stay in one city as long as the fans demanded another show.

All of his touring plans were put on hold, however, in 1993. In April 1993, Brooks said he was taking an eight-month break from music. He wanted to spend time with his wife and new daughter, Taylor May Pearl. He was not worried about being away from his fans for that time. "Whether the people are there or not after I come off of the eight months is a chance that we take," he said. "But I feel that's a chance I must take."

Jimmy Bowen, Capitol Nashville's president, had no doubts about Brooks' future. "You're going to see him succeed because he's got his head on straight," he said. "He's got some very creative ideas on how to reach people."

Brooks is just happy to be doing what he loves. During one interview, he looked back to the very beginning of his career. "The first trip to Nashville was worth it," he said. "All the heartaches I have suffered because I have chosen music over other things is worth it."

Garth Brooks as he stands with his award
for Top Male Country Singer of the Year, 1993.

GARTH BROOKS' ADDRESS

For more information about Garth Brooks and to subscribe to the fan magazine *The Believer,* write to:

The Believer Magazine
P.O. Box 507
Goodlettsville, TN 37070-0507

If you want to receive a reply, enclose a self-addressed stamped envelope with your letter.